TREASURED AND
TEACHABLE

Books by Elizabeth Bauman

Hope's Colors
Homeschooling Hope
Treasured and Teachable

TREASURED AND TEACHABLE

Homeschooling to College with
Hope, Joy and Asperger's

ELIZABETH BAUMAN

To Mama, who loved teaching
and always saw the potential in people

Contents

Introduction

Years ago, I sat in a parent-teacher conference. The news was not good and I had to face some discouraging facts. My daughter, Katie, has Asperger's Syndrome. She had failing grades in reading and spelling and was unable to understand instructions. Her public elementary school teacher described her as a struggling student who was socially awkward. Katie was sometimes disruptive. Teacher expectations were not high. The evidence suggested Katie should remain in special ed classes with a full-time para-professional. Hearing this, our family made a bold decision that changed our lives.

Perhaps your child struggles in public school and is not making satisfactory progress. Have you ever wondered, as we did, if there was a better way to learn? Do you want something more for your son or daughter?

This is the story of our homeschooling journey from special ed classrooms to college scholarships. Our adventures took us far beyond the walls of home. We learned alongside dozens of other families who became our friends. Through a kaleidoscope of fun and creative classes, Katie discovered a passion for learning. With increasing faith and determination, she accomplished what some thought she could never do.

My purpose in writing *Treasured and Teachable* is to give you hope and a road map. The book reveals the pros and cons of homeschooling, our failures as well as our accomplishments, to help enhance your educational journey. Learn how you can enjoy these precious school years with your children and help them reach their full potential. Amazing things can happen when you look beyond test results, trust God, and take a step of faith.

This book will show you how to connect with other homeschool families to get the support you need. No one understands the challenges you face like an experienced home educator. I was fortunate to know a number of former public school teachers who chose to homeschool their own children. They provided a wealth of information. When you are homeschooling, you need all the help and encouragement you can get.

Homeschooling allows you the freedom to choose your curriculum and educational experiences, and to customize learning to your child's needs and interests. This book suggests many websites to help you find the right curriculum and access educational materials. You are not limited to a standard text-book-based and schedule-bound education at home. You will learn about hybrid homeschooling through our experiences with a co-op, private learning centers, church and community programs, and online instruction. If one educational approach doesn't work for your child, you are free to try another.

Homeschooling does not have to be expensive. Some parents homeschool their children for free using online classes. Some teach in lieu of private school tuition or volunteer in a co-op. Field trips are an affordable and fun way to learn. I will share ways your family can save money and still provide a great education.

There are many wonderful benefits from participating in extracurricular activities. These include making friends, gaining confidence, developing a skill, learning teamwork, giving back to the community, and so forth. I share our involvement in Scouts, sports, church groups and community service organizations to show you how participation may help your child.

Finally, the book will help you prepare your teenager for college or career. There are classes required to graduate from high school. Your child may take more challenging classes if he plans to attend college. You will learn how to prepare students for the SAT or ACT, qualify for dual enrollment, and look for college scholarships. A solid high school education prepares students for whatever path they may choose.

The events in this book are true, but some names and details have been changed to protect identities.

"Why fit in when you were born to stand out?"

Dr. Seuss

Chapter One
The Question

"Don't you want her to be like everyone else?"

I was stunned by the school counselor's question. Why would I want any child to be like everyone else? Shouldn't we value people for who they are?

My eleven-year-old daughter, Katie, had outbursts when she felt overwhelmed. She had trouble following directions. She could be difficult to understand and she didn't make friends easily. But be like everyone else? That was doubtful. Katie has Asperger's Syndrome.

I wanted Katie to be herself. She loved to paint in bright swirling colors and design floor plans. She built amazing structures out of recycled materials. She won first place in the school art competition every year. She enjoyed exploring and being outdoors. She had a creative and courageous spirit that no educational box could contain.

The counselor asked more questions. So did Katie's teacher. I was still not sure how to respond. I wondered what was best for my daughter. What were her options? She could remain in special ed at the public elementary school. She had a good teacher and a wonderful para-professional, but Katie was unhappy there. She struggled to complete the daily homework on time and disliked the books they were reading. She was bored and didn't understand the rules. She spent most of her recess periods in study hall, finishing daily assignments and thinking of ways to escape. One day she made it halfway out the window before the teacher stopped her. School bullies taunted her. One day, a boy on the bus hit her with a lunch box. Classmates excluded her.

The public school was simply not a good fit for my daughter. We couldn't afford private school without getting a sizable loan. I doubted Katie would do much better there. Finally, there was the option to homeschool, but I knew very little about that.

I felt overwhelmed just thinking about teaching Katie at home. I had trouble explaining how to load a dishwasher. Did I honestly want to tackle fifth-grade science? Then there was math. I was absent the week they covered square roots. What about socialization? I was not that outgoing mom who entertains on a regular basis. Only because Katie was failing to thrive in public school did I even consider home education.

I talked with my husband, Roy, and our two children and explained that I could teach Katie at home. After a long pause, my ten-year-old son asked, "Mom, are you sure you're smart enough?" My husband frowned at him, but I thought maybe Bobby had a point. The previous week, I washed his pants with a crayon in the pocket and left my purse at the grocery store.

I looked up Georgia homeschool requirements on the internet. I read several books, including *Homeschooling for Excellence* and *The Well-trained Mind: A Guide to Classical Education at Home.* Learning had always been my passion and I hoped to find a way to share that joy with my child. Would I regret it more if I tried homeschooling and failed, or if I never attempted it at all?

Roy and I prayed about the decision and discussed it with our daughter. We agreed to withdraw Katie from public school. We believed she needed more freedom to reach her highest potential. We wanted an educational program that fit her well and allowed her to maximize her greatest strengths. She needed to move at her own pace, academically and socially. We hoped and prayed she would become the best she could possibly be. We were not sure how that would happen, but we had faith.

Do you feel the same way? Is your child not living up to his or her potential? What can you do?

There are many things to consider before removing your child from public school. Homeschooling is a huge time commitment. Are you prepared to teach your son or daughter? If necessary, can your family survive on one income? Is your spouse in complete agreement and will he or she contribute to the task? Will any relatives or friends lend a hand? Do you know other homeschool families in your area who will assist you? Will home learning work well for your child? You can't know for sure until you try. If things don't go well at home, your child can always return to public school.

Does your child need support services, such as speech-language therapy, from the local school? If you homeschool a child with special needs, you may have the right to free evaluations and an Individualized Education Program (IEP) team. Some state schools may make support services available to homeschooled students. You may have to decide whether to use public services or switch to private sources. The Home School Legal Defense Association (HSLDA) recommends that parents of special needs children arrange for regular evaluations and document their child's progress. They suggest standardized achievement tests, such as the Iowa Test of Basic

Skills (ITBS), and psycho-educational testing conducted by a licensed professional. You may visit hslda.org for more information. The HSLDA can help you arrange for any services and evaluations your child may need.

There are many considerations that go into whether to homeschool. It is a decision based on your child's needs, what is best for her or him, and your family circumstances. Read on for more guidance in making the decisions you face.

"For I know the plans I have
for you," declares the Lord,
"plans to prosper you and not
to harm you, plans to give
you hope and a future."

Jeremiah 29:11 NIV

Chapter Two
The Journey Begins

How hard could it be? I filed my intent to homeschool and we got started. Katie and I sat down at the kitchen table with a complete school-in-a-box curriculum from a local home-school book store. I figured we should do math from 9:00–10:00, language arts from 10:00–11:00, science from 11:00–12:00, and social studies after lunch. Why not follow the public school schedule?

I soon realized that Katie was indeed below grade level in reading and had trouble spelling and writing. The curriculum was too demanding for her and she was unable to finish the daily language arts assignment in an hour. She disliked reading. I felt like I had jumped from the frying pan into the fire.

By the end of the first week, Katie was confused, and I was binge-eating chocolate. It was 3:00 on Friday afternoon and I was still in my pajamas. We still had seven years, eight months and ten days to go before Katie graduated. Teaching a fifth-grader at home, especially mine, was like stumbling down a wooded path in the dark without a flashlight.

Why was this so difficult? I had faced greater challenges. I thought back to when Katie was two years old and first diagnosed with autism spectrum disorder. The psychiatrist said she was "in her own little world." Her speech and behavior were not age appropriate. Katie saw several specialists and their reports were not encouraging. I took her to speech and occupational therapists three times a week with her baby brother in tow. Then, a few months after hearing Katie's diagnosis, I received my own. I had stage two, level four malignant melanoma. The oncologist told me that only 35% of patients like me survive five years. By God's grace, Katie and I exceeded professional expectations.

Katie's speech improved, she learned how to read and she began to interact with others. She developed a passion for art. I was now a ten-year cancer survivor. Given all this, why was I suddenly feeling discouraged?

I was stuck at home. I felt isolated and completely frustrated. I already wanted to quit homeschooling, but I sensed I shouldn't give up so quickly. I prayed for help and direction. I needed confirmation we were doing the right thing. I needed wisdom and patience. I needed all the help I could get.

Two weeks later, a friend invited me to a home educator's meeting. My limited perspective was about to expand and reach far beyond the four walls of our kitchen, a rigid schedule, and that intimidating stack of school books.

"Everybody is a genius. But if you judge a fish by its ability to climb a tree, it will live its whole life believing that it is stupid."

Albert Einstein

Chapter Three

The Homeschool Support Group

What is the best way to homeschool a child with Asperger's Syndrome? How do you teach any child who learns differently? What was I doing wrong? I was about to get some answers.

Thirty-four homeschooling moms gathered in a neighbor's family room. At least ten of them were former public school teachers. Susan, the speaker, was an experienced educator who taught children with special needs. She looked beyond physical or mental disabilities. She believed all children have a gift or talent worthy of developing. She said every child is a unique treasure. I liked her immediately.

Susan discussed the many advantages of home education. It allows one-on-one instruction tailored to the individual child. Students learn at their own pace. There is no need to move on until they have mastered each lesson. She explained how to teach our children in a way that fits their learning style. Some students learn best by reading textbooks. Others do well watching DVDs or online tutorials. Some pupils love playing computer games. Or they may favor a hands-on approach such as science experiments or using blocks to learn math.

Is your child's preferred learning style visual, auditory, or kinesthetic? There is a free learning style quiz on Howtolearn. com. If your child is like mine, you tell her something and she soon forgets. However, if she sees a picture or makes something, she remembers.

Susan offered tips to make learning fun. We can sing songs to memorize facts. Children can draw or paint what they hear. They can play games, build things, or put on puppet shows. Students can spend more time learning outdoors. They can listen to music or discuss interesting topics with classmates. Young children learn best by playing and doing activities they enjoy.

Finally, the speaker discussed hybrid homeschooling. This involved taking some classes outside the home. No one parent is qualified to teach every subject and children need to spend time with others. She encouraged us to go to a learning center, educational co-op, or community facility. We could take private music or art lessons. If necessary, we could hire a tutor. Families could select the class, learning style, time of day, and teacher best suited for their child. Students could also learn online. After the homeschool support group meeting, I asked Susan how to improve Katie's social skills.

My daughter does not pick up on social cues easily and is confused by verbal directions. Loud noises upset her. Susan suggested I try role playing. By pretending to be on the playground or at the grocery store, Katie would be better prepared when she got together with others. She could practice proper behavior until it became more natural. She might understand what was expected of her by acting it out.

The speaker confirmed that the earlier you begin intervention, the better it is for a child on the autism spectrum. Up to this point, Katie's progress was the result of many years of speech therapy, occupational therapy, sensory and auditory integration therapy. We even tried horseback riding and soothing music to help calm her. We continued various types of treatment as long as it benefited Katie.

Special-learning.com empowers parents of children with autism by teaching them to use Applied Behavior Analysis (ABA). Some consider ABA the world's most effective early intervention therapy. Autismspeaks.org provides a lot of information on helping those with autism spectrum disorder. They also offer inspirational stories.

Since my daughter already had problems socializing, I worried homeschooling might make it worse. I asked the parents attending the meeting what they thought. All said their children have more of a social life now than they did in public school. Their sons and daughters had time for Scouts and sports because they weren't weighed down with homework. Some children joined the local homeschool band or participated in the Science Olympiad. Homeschoolers took monthly field trips and did projects together. Many parents felt if homeschool wasn't fun, they were doing something wrong. I was happy to hear this and immediately signed Katie up for several activities. I felt new hope.

At the next support group meeting, another speaker discussed how homeschooling helps children reach their highest potential. Her own daughter went on to get a Ph.D. from Princeton at the age of twenty-three! Several in the audience shared homeschool success stories. Gail left public school in the twelfth grade so she could spend more time practicing piano and traveling to auditions around the country. She was eventually accepted to Juillard. At sixteen, Cathy had the chance to attend the School of American Ballet. Being home educated helped her achieve her dream of dancing in New York City. One lady had homeschooled eight children. Four of them were now attending very selective colleges. A sixth-grade girl was writing her own blog.

These stories inspired me. The children they described were exceptional. Like Katie, they were gifted in some way. I saw that children's unique gifts and abilities were easily overlooked in a large public school setting. Home education gave children more opportunities to shine and the time to pursue their passions.

While greatly encouraged by this group, I also felt a bit intimidated. Could I possibly measure up to these amazing parents? Thankfully, this was not a science fair and I did not have to compete. These homeschooling moms were a great blessing to me. They provided the affirmation I craved. I was thrilled to have their guidance and emotional support. I wasn't alone in my journey and neither was Katie. They introduced me to the wide world of homeschooling, which reaches far beyond anything I imagined. It offers so much more than a standard textbook-based and schedule-bound education.

If you want to find a homeschool support group in your area, begin by asking friends or neighbors. Many large churches and community centers will help you connect with other families. Perhaps you live in a small town or a remote area. You may want to join an online homeschool community. Homeschool.com provides a great database of organizations and support groups around the United States. So does nationalhomeschoolassociation.com. There are also homeschool groups on Facebook.

If you are interested in online learning, there are a number of great websites to help you get started. These include allinonehomeschool.com and thehomeschoolmom.com. Time4Learning.com provides an award-winning online curriculum for PreK-12th grade. Khanacademy.org offers

10,000 free YouTube videos on a wide range of topics. It provides expert-created resources for every academic subject and level. K12.com offers tuition-free online public schools as well as three accredited private schools. This website provides individualized learning and teacher support. Two of the most popular sites for educational games are funbrain.com and coolmath.com.

If you want more specific information on homeschooling a child who has Asperger's Syndrome or other learning disabilities, Time4learning.com and a2zhomeschooling .com offer great suggestions and resources. Other websites are 7sistershomeschool.com, SallieBorrink.com and learndifferently.com. These sites offer great tips on how to allow students to learn at their own pace, make lessons feel like games, build study programs around the child's own interests and get children involved in their community. These ideas certainly worked for our family. Check them out to find ones that might work for yours.

"A wise teacher
makes learning a joy."

Proverbs 15:2 TLB

Chapter Four
Joyful Learning

How could I help Katie develop a passion for learning? Could I make school fun? I desperately wanted to become the best teacher I could be.

My own love of education started when I was young. I credit my mother. When I was four, Mama and I started playing a game she called "consibilities." Every morning, Mama transformed our dining room into a temporary classroom. On the table, she laid out a smorgasbord of paper, finger paint, crayons, and Play-doh. We made puppets out of lunch bags and socks. We used board games, Lincoln Logs, and Tinker Toys. Brightly colored plastic letters formed something magical called the alphabet. With these letters, Mama told me, I could make any word that came to mind. I was fascinated with the sound of each and the potential that lay with an *A*, *B* or *C*. I learned that the configuration of these letters had the power to entertain, inform, or persuade.

Every day, after Daddy went to work, my mother and I got busy with our "consibilities" by reading, drawing, exploring, and playing games. I was excited to see what I could create with a box of crayons or discover in the pages of a book or find growing in the back yard. Mama was my first and favorite teacher. She made learning fun. She gave me a passion for knowledge that I wanted to pass on to my own children. I wished I could be more like her.

During the first year that I homeschooled Katie, I called Mama often. She was a retired public school teacher and our biggest cheerleader. Her wonderful gift of encouragement was recognized by high school students who voted her "teacher of the year" in 1983. Mama saw that Katie had talent and inspired her to focus on art, her great love. We arranged for my daughter to take painting and drawing classes at the local community art center. Katie became increasingly creative and she flourished there. Mama also stressed the importance of reading aloud to improve Katie's speech and vocabulary as well as to stretch her imagination. I treasured my mother's advice and support.

At the end of that school year, my mom was diagnosed with stage four lung cancer. She would not survive another month. Mama asked to see her grandchildren and her face brightened the moment they entered her hospital room. For the next hour, she delighted us with her funny stories. She told my children and their cousins about the girl who searched everywhere for boogley boogley ice cream. Mama shared that she got into trouble for starting leaf fires as a teenager and the time her father threw flapjacks out of a farmhouse window to the pigs waiting below. She told tales about our magical childhood car that could never pass a Dairy Queen without pulling in. The grandchildren also heard about the fairy who lived in the breadbox. Mama's frail body lay confined to a hospital bed, beaten by a terminal illness. But joy prevailed that hour. One story followed another and laughter filled her room.

My mother taught our family the most valuable lessons. Mama showed us how to live in joy and walk in love, precious lessons that can only be learned outside the walls of a class-room. She saw the potential in people. She made us feel we could do anything. She encouraged us to continue our home-school journey.

Keeping your joy while homeschooling can be hard, especially when you feel isolated as well as discouraged. Prayer, talking with a close friend or relative, walking in the woods, and music can help. So can a support group or Bible study. Slow down and don't try to do four or five things at one time. Count your blessings, even after your child has a meltdown and you feel like crying. There are many online sources of support. Crosswalk.com is a Christian website offering devotionals and homeschooling encouragement and resources. TheHomeschoolmom.com also provides tips and inspiration. Myjoyfilledlife.com offers an online conference to encourage the home educator.

Laughter is the best medicine. I love the homeschool comic strips on Pinterest and *The Official Book of Homeschooling Cartoons* by Todd Wilson. Some homeschool YouTube videos are hilarious. It's a relief to know I'm not the only home educator who makes dumb mistakes or has a child act inappropriately. After years of homeschooling, I tell my own funny stories about embarrassing moments.

Don't lose your joy.

"Whether you think you can or
think you can't, you're right."

Henry Ford

Chapter Five
The Homeschool Expo

It was my first time at a homeschool expo. I felt like a kid at a carnival with a pocketful of tickets. My homeschool mentor, Juanita, and I entered the grand lobby of the Cobb Galleria Centre and rode the escalator to the second floor. Inside the cavernous meeting rooms were nearly one hundred booths hosted by dozens of vendors. I had so much to learn about homeschooling. Where should I go first? Could I get Katie through the sixth grade? Juanita was a public school teacher and was now homeschooling her two children through high school. She told me I could do this.

I decided to look at different textbooks to find the best fit for my daughter. There were dozens of publishers offering educational materials for homeschoolers. Several of the leading homeschool publishers were there. I hurried over to their tables and bought several books. I also found math DVDs. These would work beautifully for Katie.

One of the most difficult tasks is choosing the right homeschool curriculum for your child. Thehomeschoolmom .com, Cathyduffyreviews.com and thecurriculumchoice.com provide curriculum reviews to help you choose. I highly recommend *101 Top Picks for Homeschool Curriculum* by Cathy Duffy. Another approach is to ask friends who homeschool what they use and see if you can borrow or buy their used books. You want a curriculum that matches your family's educational philosophy and one that fits your child's learning style. You can decide if you want everything done for you or you would rather design your own lesson plans.

In selecting a curriculum, you need to consider your child's strengths and weaknesses. For instance, your child might watch math DVDs where an experienced teacher explains how to do pre-algebra problems. The child could play these over and over again until he mastered each math concept. You could use a textbook-based curriculum for language arts, reading, and history. The child could take drawing and painting classes at the community art center. He could take science classes at a private school with a certified teacher. If one curriculum doesn't work for your child, then try something else.

While at the expo, I learned more about community organizations. I stopped by to talk to representatives from the Girl Scouts, Atlanta Symphony Orchestra, Georgia State Parks, the YMCA, Fox Theatre, and Zoo Atlanta. These groups offered excellent suggestions for field trips and extracurricular activities. We discussed sports programs and volunteer opportunities. If you are interested, Homeschoolsuccess.com and thehomeschoolmom.com also provide a list of great activities for homeschoolers.

Juanita had some questions about the legal aspects of education so we visited the Home School Legal Defense Association (HSLDA) table. We learned homeschooling is legal in all fifty states, but state guidelines vary. HSLDA told me about the educational requirements for Georgia. Juanita was moving out west soon and she asked about Arizona's academic standards. Their website is hslda.org and they protect the freedom to homeschool in the United States and around the world. I learned homeschooling is illegal in some countries. I am thankful that Americans have the right to teach their own children.

Two dozen speakers offered workshops on a variety of topics. I was eager to attend and learn about standardized test prep and how to homeschool for free using the internet. There were also classes on time management and teaching techniques for students with special needs.

Do most colleges accept homeschooled students? I saw admissions officers from six or seven southern colleges at the expo. I was pleased to learn that most schools, even Ivy League colleges, accept homeschoolers. A large number offer online college classes for high school upperclassmen. Several local learning academies and private secondary schools also provide classes. I was happy there were so many opportunities, but I wondered if Katie would ever be ready for college.

The Southeast Homeschool Expo is one of the largest in the region and is held every summer. I stopped by dozens of tables and received great advice from experienced educators and community volunteers. They answered all my homeschooling questions. It was certainly worth the visit. Surrounded by hundreds of fellow homeschoolers, I felt like part of something grand and glorious. Their enthusiasm was contagious. I left believing my daughter and I could make it through middle school.

You can learn more about this three-day convention at southeasthomeschoolexpo.com. There are other homeschool conferences held all across the United States. Maybe one will be right for you.

"I took the pieces you threw away,
put them together by night and day.
Washed by the rain.
Dried by the sun.
A million pieces all in one."

Howard Finster

Chapter Six
Katie's Kaleidoscope

Would Katie be pleased or disappointed?

I held my breath as our family walked into the enormous exhibition hall at the north Georgia state fair. Gorgeous hand-made quilts were suspended from the rafters. Dozens of tables displayed thousands of items, including floral arrangements, handmade dresses, and framed photographs. Our eyes darted from a cabinet filled with canned preserves to a counter covered with crocheted blankets. We glanced at pottery-filled shelves as we walked through the building. The back wall was decorated with hundreds of children's drawings and paintings. Their art work reflected their dreams, creativity, and talent. My eyes scanned the pictures and then settled on Katie's painting of a log cabin at sunset. It wore a blue ribbon!

One of my favorite things about homeschooling was having time for Katie to create art. Working at her own pace, Katie usually finished her core classwork in three or four hours. This gave her an entire afternoon to pursue her passion for drawing, painting, and making crafts. She had time to build model homes and doll furniture out of twigs she gathered in the back yard. She also used bottle caps, glass beads, and small pieces of plastic. At the next state fair, she won first place for a life-size, free-standing figure she constructed out of multi-colored popsicle sticks. Her art projects were a kaleidoscope of colorful creations.

Homeschooling allows more time to pursue individual interests and develop a particular talent. Children can be as creative as they like. What does your child dream of doing? What are his or her gifts and talents?

Even after our first two years of home education, I still celebrated the fact we had so much freedom and flexibility. We set our own schedules and traveled when we pleased. Katie took personal enrichment classes at two local churches. She took swimming and cooking lessons at the nearby YMCA. We designed our own curriculum tailored to Katie's strengths and interests. Unit studies worked well during fifth grade. At that age, Katie loved American Girl dolls. We found books about these dolls and she suddenly became excited about reading. She wrote book reports on American Girl stories. I taught history lessons based on the time periods in which the dolls lived. We had tea parties with her dolls and read Katie's favorite stories aloud.

If you are interested, you can design unit studies based on sailing ships or desert animals or any other topic that fascinates your child. Cathyduffyreviews.com offers resources to help you create your own unit studies or you can use existing studies. Autisticmama.com provides a plan for a year of homeschool unit studies.

I loved that we belonged to a wonderful educational community. We made new friends. Fellow homeschoolers were eager to help and encourage us. We were involved in church recreational programs. Our homeschool group participated in science fairs, the Science Olympiad, Living History Day, and other community events. Katie joined the group every month for field trips and community service projects. In most cities, there are a number of homeschool groups as well as special needs support groups. You may also join online organizations.

Katie's brother, Bobby, also joined us in our homeschooling adventure. In public school, he was drowning in a sea of homework every night. He was frustrated and discouraged. Bobby has Centralized Auditory Processing Disorder and a large, noisy classroom is distracting. His report card was less than stellar. When I pictured my son at age five, I saw him smiling as he kicked a soccer ball. At ten, I saw him grinning as he hit the baseball out of the park. But the mental snapshot I had of him at twelve was sitting there looking miserable at 11:00 p.m., his desk covered by a dozen school books and a stack of homework assignments. At thirteen, Bobby thought it best to leave all that behind and join us in our educational journey.

While homeschooling, we participated in extracurricular activities. There are many benefits to this. These include making friends, learning teamwork, staying fit, gaining confidence, and giving back to the community. These activities help develop artistic talents as well as communication and leadership skills. Katie and Bobby participated in a number of group activities such as sports, Scouts, art camp, and youth group. The amount of homework they had was about half of what it was in public school, so there was time for these pursuits.

I was fortunate that my husband played a part in our home-based adventure. Roy didn't teach, but he helped coach our children's baseball and basketball teams. He also drove the kids to dances and helped with Scout projects. Roy listened while I vented about daily challenges and he offered practical solutions. We all traveled and learned together during our road trips. Homeschooling was a family affair.

Does this sound too good to be true? Keep reading.

"I have NOT failed.
I've just found 10,000 ways
that won't work."

Thomas Edison

Chapter Seven
Not Every Day
Is Perfect

Nothing had gone according to plan and it was only August. A few days earlier, a neighbor and I had backed out of our driveways at the same time and crashed, smack dab in the middle of the road. My car was finally out of the shop, but now our air conditioning was broken. That morning, I took Katie and Bobby to the lake. They found a large makeshift plastic raft and climbed aboard. Within minutes, it drifted out into the middle of the wide, deep lake. As I watched, a current carried them across the water to the opposite side where they were finally able to swim to shore. Because of that episode, Katie missed her art class. Later, halfway to basketball practice, Katie said, "Uh Oh! My shoes don't match."

Things happened to wreak havoc with our schedule. Katie and Bobby got head lice. One day, we desperately needed a plumber and waited hours for him to arrive. Often, we had a huge mess in our kitchen because a science experiment went wrong. For these and other reasons, it was hard to stick to a daily plan.

Home education required a huge time commitment. It was

a full-time, demanding and unpaid position. There was little time apart from my children. I was a full-time chauffeur. I missed lunches with friends and having a paid job. Come February, all of us felt completely burned out. On one particularly tough day, dinner was a bag of corn chips.

Homeschooling required patience. I sometimes lost it after explaining the same lesson thirteen times. There were things my kids did not want to learn. I even tried to get them to like Shakespeare by reading *Hamlet* aloud using funny foreign accents. I repeated things over and over again and no one seemed to be listening. I got tired of trying to convince some extended family members that I was not delusional and homeschooling was actually legal. They didn't understand why my children weren't in public school like everyone else. I may have had a master's degree in education, but they thought I was crazy for wanting to go against the grain.

My husband was not bothered by others' opinions. He told me "the pioneers take the arrows." He supported our family financially as well as emotionally. Sometimes we struggled to make ends meet, but God always provided the jobs Roy needed. Being self-employed while homeschooling required a certain amount of courage.

A friend asked me how I kept my house clean while homeschooling and the answer was, I don't. Dishes piled up in the sink and the laundry basket was usually overflowing. Dinner was rarely on the table by 6:00 p.m. As my children get older, I finally realized I could have them do housework as credit for home economics.

One of the major objections people have to homeschooling is lack of socialization. I constantly needed to reassure relatives, friends, and neighbors that my kids interacted with others. I shared that Bobby and Katie had friends and participated in a variety of community activities. Ironically, my children did more socializing as homeschoolers than when they were in public school.

As my children approached high school, I faced the mountain of teaching science and math. I was simply not equipped to be a chemistry or calculus instructor. I'd forgotten how to do algebra. I struggled with anything mechanical and would not dissect an animal under any circumstances. For those and other reasons, Roy and I enrolled Katie and Bobby in a home studies learning center. I hoped that conditions would improve.

To keep moving forward when everything was falling apart, I had to remember my dream for my children's future. What if Thomas Edison had given up on the light bulb just one day before he discovered how to make it work? In the future, I'd probably look back and actually miss these times together. During the most chaotic afternoons, I just ended the school day early. We would make a large pan of brownies or go out for ice cream.

When people asked me why my children weren't in public school, I just bit my tongue and smiled. I'd think of Mark Twain's words, "I have never let my schooling interfere with my education," and we'd go on our way. I couldn't let other people's opinions keep me from doing what I believed was best.

Home education is not for everyone, but it worked for us.

"Men love to wonder, and that is
the seed of science."

Ralph Waldo Emerson

Chapter Eight
The Supafunjacational Learning Center

"Alright, guys. Bring it in and we'll see what we have."

Waist-deep in the ocean, Bobby and five other middle-schoolers were seining for sea creatures. Following instructions, they pulled a huge net onto shore and a large crowd gathered around them.

"Great catch!" said the student leader, as they all peered into the net. "There's two kinds of fish, three horseshoe crabs, a starfish, and some shrimp. OK, put them in buckets of water so you can count and measure them. Remember to record everything in your notebooks. We'll release them when you're finished. The next group will go out soon."

I sat on the beach with approximately 200 seventh and eighth graders, at least twenty fellow chaperones, and staff members from the home studies learning center. It was a gorgeous April afternoon and we were on the Georgia coast for a week-long expedition.

After lunch, the students went back to the beach to create sand sculptures. Each group designed amazing sand art. They sculpted a giant alligator, a sea turtle, and a dozen other creatures. Before the day was over, the younger students watched as the high school seniors dissected a small animal. They drew and diagramed what they observed. They had a kite-flying competition before they went swimming. Later, they participated in humorous skits. "Supafunjacational" was a word Katie made up to describe the fun educational activities. There was never a dull moment.

I walked along the shore as the sun set and the sea sparkled. A group of girls were coming toward me, skipping along the water's edge. My daughter was in the center with two girls on both sides of her, arms linked. They were all laughing and Katie looked radiant. She'd made new friends, ones she would have for years. I snapped a quick candid photo and caught the light circling Katie's head and her spectacular smile. I captured that moment on film, and in my heart, forever.

We first heard about this home studies learning center from several homeschooling moms. The center offered a range of classes, but the primary focus was science. Not science as I learned it through textbooks and lectures. This was hands-on, roll up your sleeves, dig in the dirt and experience our wonderful world kind of science. It was there my daughter developed a deep passion for learning and found pure joy in discovering the world around her.

The learning center was an incredible blessing to our family. There were so many wonderful educational experiences there. My children's spirit of wonder and imagination soared. My children gave their seventh grade class presentation on a disease they researched. In eighth grade, they built toothpick bridges that supported over fifty pounds. Students conducted dozens of science experiments and kept a journal of their activities. It got even better in high school. Students built a Rube Goldberg machine and took robotics classes. Katie and her classmates dissected six animals, including a cat. Her physics class constructed a trebuchet, a type of catapult, on the center's large open field.

Bobby certainly benefited from the two years he spent there. He loved the hands-on approach to science and the chance to study outdoors. He formed friendships by working on projects and playing sports outside with his classmates. Bobby became interested in recycling and developed a deep respect for our planet. Centralized Auditory Processing Disorder was not an issue for him there as it had been in crowded, noisy classrooms. He also enjoyed more flexibility. In public school classrooms, everyone learns at one pace and works on the same tasks, five days a week. Instead, Bobby went to the home studies learning center one day a week for several hours. He had more freedom to select projects and complete assignments in his own time during the week. This was a great way for him to learn time management.

Katie especially loved the science classes at the learning center. She remained there for five years. She expressed her gratitude to the school's directors in a letter. She wrote, "I am so glad you care so much about me to make me feel like I'm very special. I'm at home in my beloved school. Thank you so much for having this place where I can freely express my creativity and unlock my full learning potential. I never in my whole life saw a place that is anything like it. I love how you don't go with the status quo. You make students like me feel special by teaching us in a very creative, unique and supafun-jacational way. Thank you so much for creating this wonderful environment that is a perfect fit for me. I have made so many friends here.

"I loved studying the complexity of a cell and how trillions of proteins all work together in harmony within a tiny section of the plasma membrane. It made me realize how I am wonderfully made and that God loves me just as I am. All my classes opened a window into a wonderland in my heart. I can now see a doorway leading to the light of God's marvelous presence."

How do you choose the best learning center for your child? Start by asking homeschoolers you know. Visit a few centers in your area. You may know from the first open house if your children would be happy there. Does the school's educational philosophy match your own? Are the teachers well-qualified? Is the center highly recommended by other homeschool families? Are the online reviews favorable? Is the facility safe and well-maintained? Sit in on a class and observe the teaching style. Are the students friendly or are there cliques? Are there many disciplinary problems? Does your child like the teacher? After visiting several schools, you will know when you've found the right one for your family.

"Your talent is God's gift to you. What you do with it is your gift back to God."

Leo Buscaglia

Chapter Nine
The Kaleidoscopic Co-op

About 300 people sat in the audience at the community arts center. The lights were dimmed and the theater curtains parted. A couple of minutes later, my daughter appeared on stage. Katie was cast as the student in *The Seuss Odyssey*. My husband and I were nervous for her, but Katie appeared to be perfectly at ease. She memorized all of her lines and delivered them beautifully throughout the play. Here she was at fourteen, speaking clearly, making no discernible mistakes, poised, and confident. I thanked God for her amazing transformation!

For ten years, Katie's therapists advised us to keep taking baby steps and to celebrate the victories, however small. This became our life philosophy. We handled life one day at a time. We had faith and hoped for the best. We rejoiced in each other's milestones. Now here we were, in the community arts center, enjoying Katie's performance and realizing that all things are possible with God.

This play was presented by a local homeschool co-op. We had joined eight months before, while still taking science classes at the learning center. This co-op was formed by friends who thought it would be more fun to teach their children together rather than separately at home. The group included almost 100 parent-teachers, representing a wide variety of occupations as well as talents and abilities. Each parent volunteered to teach or work in their area of expertise for at least five hours each week. Two ladies with community theater experience started the drama class. We had an engineer teaching an algebra class and a nurse leading a health seminar. A mom from Venezuela taught Spanish. Professional artists offered painting and drawing classes. All of the teachers focused on developing their students' talents. They made learning fun.

My favorite co-op event was the end-of-the year talent show. In this performance, every student had the opportunity to showcase their talents in front of their classmates, parents, and teachers. Katie and Jessica sang and played guitar. Kylie and Sam tap danced. Sarah painted onstage, and eight students participated in a skit one of them had written. Bobby worked behind the scenes and helped set up the stage. Eric played the piano, and Nathan entertained us with magic tricks. John performed the dance from *Napoleon Dynamite*. Every child had the chance to be a star that afternoon.

Is a co-op the right option for your family? Do you enjoy teaching other children? Do you have a favorite subject or special talent you want to share? Or would you be more comfortable preparing lunch, working in the nursery, cleaning, or serving at the administration table? Fortunately, there is a job to fit every parent involved in a homeschool co-op.

For our first year in the co-op, I decided to teach a third-grade Bible class, a fifth-grade language arts class, and a sixth-grade math class. The eight-year-olds were sweet. I loved reading books to them and helping them make crafts. We had fun in the language arts class penning haikus and writing stories.

We often walked to a nearby library to check out books. I enjoyed teaching the elementary school students.

Teaching the middle school students made me nervous. There were eight boys. Most of them were smarter than I am, and they knew they were smarter. They grew up using computers and they noticed I was not tech-savvy. They thought they knew everything there was to know about math. I decided to ask students to volunteer to teach lessons. There were a couple of boys who were knowledgeable and wanted to do this. Some of the more advanced students even offered to help classmates solve math problems.

If the middle school students got too full of themselves, I threw out big words to see what they would say. Sometimes, I resorted to hippopotomonstrosesquipedalianism (using very long words) to get respect. On April Fool's Day, I told them I knew Thomas Edison personally because we went to school together. I was in my fifties then, so some of them believed me and started to pay attention. It was the last year I taught middle school math. I much preferred reading and writing to solving pre-algebra problems.

When I think back to our years in the homeschool co-op, a kaleidoscope of images floods my mind. I can still see the stars at the overnight camping trip, the children sitting around the bonfire, swimming in the lake, or hearing stories told in a gigantic teepee. I remember canned food drives and helping distribute toys before Christmas. There were trips downtown to the Holocaust museum and the Shakespeare Tavern. I can picture the dance classes where young people waltzed or line danced across the gym. Then there was the trip to a Florida beach. The scenes changed through the years, with new places and people, creating fresh and beautiful patterns, each lovely in its own way.

Can you picture your child in a homeschool co-op? Are these the sort of events your child would enjoy? Would you enjoy working alongside other parents?

We met so many amazing people through this group of home educators. I will never forget the co-op's director who had the organizational and social skills to run a corporation, or the mom who homeschooled thirteen children, or the beautiful and compassionate lady who started a nonprofit to help the needy overseas. Many served as missionaries and several of these families adopted foster children. We had the great privilege to learn and work alongside them.

Our family loved the learning center and the co-op. Both places had something unique to offer, were a good match for our children, accepted students with special needs, and greatly assisted in our educational efforts. Still, we were open to additional options. If taking classes at two places was good, maybe three would be even better. So when we heard about a non-traditional school for homeschoolers located at a country church, we decided to take a look.

"We dance for laughter, we dance for tears, we dance for madness, we dance for fears, we dance for hopes, we dance for screams, we are the dancers, we create the dreams."

Albert Einstein

Chapter Ten
The Country School

It was a bright and balmy morning in May, one of those rare days that qualify as perfect. Katie, Bobby, and I drove several miles from town until we saw open green fields and more cows than cars. The non-traditional homeschooling center was located in a small church, complete with an old red barn, situated on ten wooded acres. Sometimes around dusk, when things were very quiet, you could watch deer grazing nearby.

The first thing we noticed as we pulled into the parking lot was the bright orange hot air balloon. We dashed around to the huge open field in back of the church. They were giving complimentary rides! I heard music playing and shaving-cream-covered students squealing as they flew down the hill on a long Slip 'N Slide. Some teens tossed a frisbee while others played tug-of-war. There was a softball game on an adjacent pasture. Small children were swinging on the playground and scampering across the monkey bars.

We walked inside the building. Tables were loaded to capacity with sandwiches, cupcakes, snacks and soft drinks. Youngsters were having their faces painted. Teens, clad in shorts and bathing suits, were sprawled out along the indoor hallways, talking and eating. Katie and Bobby were soon having a fabulous time celebrating the last day of the school year. I hurried outside to join my friends in the pavilion.

Of the three homeschool centers we attended, this one was the most relaxed. The energy here was friendly, accepting, and comfortable. Weather permitting, classes were often held outdoors. The school had a novel educational approach. They celebrated creativity. They encouraged students to do their own research in areas of their interest and then share what they learned with classmates. There were several children with special needs there and their moms and I formed a prayer group. They soon became my close friends.

Katie and Bobby's favorite part of this school were the weekly field trips. Students were divided into teams based on their vocational interests. Katie's group visited museums, art studios, and craft shows, while Bobby's cluster met with small business owners, sold products, and visited a local college business class. They greatly enjoyed this chance to explore possible careers.

Have you considered taking classes at a private school, but couldn't afford it? Some schools will allow you to teach or work on the grounds in lieu of tuition. Some may offer scholarships.

This school's director was willing to allow students freedom to learn differently and to give teachers flexibility in how they taught. Students worked at their own pace in the math lab using their laptops. They wrote essays and research papers on subjects of interest. They often used Khan Academy's online tutorials. One lady taught a robotics class, open to interested children as young as eight. They put together and operated small cars. I taught sixth-grade language arts and decided to use a book of vocabulary cartoons to teach my students SAT words. One student told me she would never be able to learn these words. However, she worked hard and earned a B in the class. She was proud of her accomplishment and so was I.

I helped teach a high school history class. We sometimes showed movies about historical events as well as history DVDs. For several weeks, our students watched a Harvard professor discuss ethical issues and the political philosophies on which our government is based. We then asked them what they would do in a certain situation and why. My children enjoyed these discussions. It helped them learn to think critically. They thought it was better than sitting quietly while a teacher, such as myself, lectured for an hour. Yes, some of this material was way over their heads. But we would rather aim high and get halfway there, than aim low and hit the mark.

This school had an outstanding records administrator who handled our transcript accreditation and would later help us with college applications. This was very helpful since I wanted official validation that my children were completing our state's high school graduation requirements. I did not want to spend a lot of time handling paperwork. In our area, there are a number of certified individuals who will do transcript accreditation for a reasonable price. You may search the internet to find those who accredit homeschool transcripts in your state. On the other hand, several websites tell you how to do your own homeschool transcripts for free. For example, eclectichomeschool.org offers a blank high school transcript that you may download. You may create your own homeschool transcript on howtohomeschooltoday.com. Some colleges will accept students who have a non-accredited homeschool transcript completed by a parent. Others may not.

The administrator also talked to us about dual enrollment. Georgia has a state scholarship program that pays for qualified high school students to earn college credits. It is a fantastic opportunity for teens with at least a 3.0 GPA and satisfactory

SAT or ACT scores to get a jump start on higher education. Information about Georgia's Move on When Ready/dual enrollment program is available at gafutures.org and gadoe.org. There are similar programs in other states.

It all sounded great. However, I wondered if Katie and Bobby would qualify.

"Every individual matters.
Every individual has a role
to play. Every individual
makes a difference."

Jane Goodall

Chapter Eleven
Explore the Options

Sarah's house should have been featured in a magazine. Every room was beautifully decorated. She had a cleaning lady every week and her house was immaculate. In her large finished basement, was a huge space designated as a classroom. She had desks and chairs for all three of her children as well as a chalkboard, large flat screen TV, storage shelves, and work tables. There was even a sink, mini fridge, and microwave oven nearby. Sarah was a homeschooling mom extraordinaire.

At our house, the dining room table was covered with books, Katie's drawings, colored pencils, a laptop, notebooks, and school projects as well as a couple of tennis balls. There were piles of educational DVDs in our family room along with more books and school supplies. Equipment for my children's science experiment sat on our kitchen counter. Along the walls of the stairway to my basement were pictures my children had drawn since they were old enough to pick up a crayon. On one basement wall were colorful handprints and other finger-painted works of art from preschool days. Bobby wrote out the alphabet there in bright red crayon when he was five years old. I knew I should probably repaint that wall but decided to wait. A friend saw our basement for the first time and burst out laughing. I tended to have different activities in different rooms, including the front porch, so my style was contemporary clutter.

Just as everyone has their own way of keeping house, there are many different ways to homeschool. As you've seen in previous chapters, there are different ways to learn and many effective teaching methods. Children do not have to sit around a kitchen table all day and read textbooks or study certain subjects during specific hours. They don't need to continually watch academic DVDs.

Explore the educational options. Talk to other homeschool parents and teachers. Consider different learning environments, whether inside or outside. Look at the church and community education programs in your area. Visit local homeschool learning centers and co-ops. Consider online classes. Take field trips and travel. Children can learn when they volunteer, do household chores, or get part-time jobs. Homeschooling is not one-size-fits-all. Find what works best for your family. Each child is unique and so is each family's homeschooling journey.

Our family embraced hybrid homeschooling. We tried a kaleidoscope of classes and activities. Our kids enjoyed taking classes at several places three or four days a week. One year, my children took a science course at a learning center on Monday, co-op classes on Tuesday and Thursdays, and took field trips with another school on Fridays. They completed assignments at home when they weren't in these classes. They also participated in Scouts and sports.

Some families prefer online courses offered by high schools or colleges. A popular choice in online public or private education programs is K12.com. Also, Khan Academy offers great tutorials on a wide range of topics free of charge. Other homeschoolers use educational DVDs or CDs.

Some homeschool families believe that travel is the best way to learn. The Smiths took a year off from school and work to travel around the world. The Henderson clan served as missionaries in Africa. Their children learned a foreign language and local customs by being immersed in another culture. The Rodriguez family took their twelve-year-old and sixteen-year-old on a mission trip once a year. They traveled to Guatemala, Spain, and Costa Rica. The Johnson children traveled with their parents all around the country. Whenever their father had a business meeting in California, Arizona, or Hawaii, the whole family went with him. Our family took road trips all over the United States. Our goal was to eventually visit all fifty states.

It is important for students to be involved with their community. For many, home education included weekly volunteer work or part-time jobs. Some children took frequent road trips or joined community sports teams or music programs. Older students worked part-time jobs or did internships while in high school. Bobby started his own yard work business. Daniel became active in a local political campaign. It is important for students to be involved with their community in some way. No child should be isolated.

While you have options, you do need to follow specific educational guidelines. Homeschooling is legal in all fifty states, but requirements vary from state to state. In some states, you may have to submit monthly attendance sheets, lesson plans, and letters of intent to homeschool. Students may need to take standardized tests every two or three years. Transcripts may need to be accredited. Children need to complete required classes to graduate from high school. You should check to see what your state requires before you begin.

You will need to learn how to keep academic records. You

should have a cabinet or drawers in which to keep homeschool documents. When I first started, I went a bit overboard and had eight binders containing every test my children ever took, along with all of their worksheets and a copy of the cover of every textbook they used. I kept handouts from all their extracurricular activities, every paper they ever wrote, a list of all the books they read and copies of all their progress reports from other teachers. I took hundreds of photos documenting every project they completed and event they attended. This was unnecessary. For help with homeschool record keeping, you may visit hslda.org, wikihow.com/Keep-Accurate-Homeschooling-Records, and simplehomeschool.net.

Don't let the process overwhelm you.

"The greatest wealth is health."

Virgil

Chapter Twelve
Life Skills and Healthy Habits

I watched five old episodes of *Dallas*. For lunch, I ate fried chicken, pork chops, chocolate cake, and peach cobbler topped with ice cream. I walked one block and called it a work out. It was the first day of summer vacation, so I figured I was entitled. Lord knows, I loved to eat and I watched too much television. I suspected I was not setting a good example for my children. I probably needed to make some changes.

My kids had a lot to learn, including practical life skills. A month ago, Bobby had been wearing his favorite pair of shorts when I noticed a large tear right under his back pocket. "You can't wear those with a big hole in them!" I said. A few minutes later, he was still wearing those shorts, but he had placed a large piece of duct tape over the rip. The other day, my smoke alarm went off. Katie and Bobby were cooking eggs. The burner was on high and they walked away for twenty minutes because they wanted them well done.

I believe the best classes teach practical skills that prepare children for life as adults. Our homeschool curriculum included courses like health and nutrition, personal finance for teens, auto maintenance, sewing, and cooking. These classes were offered at our co-op. We also had Bible studies, training in CPR, and babysitting. Young people never know when they might have to change a flat tire or cook dinner for their parents. Families took turns cleaning the rooms in the church co-op. Our kids learned to wipe a counter and scrub a toilet. Two teenage girls took care of babies and toddlers while their mothers taught class.

How important is diet? We had a health and nutrition class at the co-op taught by a registered nurse. She shared the importance of eating a healthy diet, including five fresh fruits and vegetables every day. Katie also followed a casein-free, gluten-free diet for many years. This diet was recommended by her developmental pediatrician and helps some children on the autism spectrum to focus better. It did seem to help Katie calm down and be more attentive.

Are there other healthy habits children need to develop? Exercise is important and was a daily part of our educational program. Are there any medications to help children on the autism spectrum or others with special needs? Of course, you need to ask your doctor.

Each child is unique and what works for some may not work well for others. We tried medication when Katie was in the second grade. Her public school teachers reported Katie was behaving like a zombie as a result, and we noticed the same thing at home. We tried several kinds her pediatrician had suggested, but eventually took her off medications because none seemed to help. We did see significant improvement in Katie's behavior over the years as a result of diet, occupational and sensory integration therapy, exercise, prayer, and the less stressful environment that homeschool offered. We thank God for this. But first, we always tried what doctors recommended to see how it worked for Katie.

For more information on Asperger's Syndrome, including symptoms and treatment, you may want to look at webmd .com. As they suggest, your child may benefit from seeing a developmental pediatrician, psychiatrist, or pediatric neurologist. Various therapists may help as well. They certainly helped Katie. Webmd.com also offers helpful information for a wide range of special needs. The American Academy of Pediatrics also offers a wealth of information at aap.org.

Homeschooled students need to learn life skills to help them make good decisions. It is important to seek advice from experienced professionals, such as doctors and therapists, when necessary.

"Somewhere inside all of us is the power to change the world."

Roald Dahl

Chapter Thirteen
Celebrate Your Child

The atmosphere was festive and the homemade cookies were delicious. A long table was covered in lace and laden with sandwiches and desserts. Teapots held various flavors of tea. About forty students, eight parents, and a few staff members gathered in a large open room at the home studies learning center. My husband and I were dressed up for this party honoring Katie and three other girls, a celebration of their sixteenth birthdays. The honorees sat at the front of the room and the guests approached them, one by one, with a small present and a card. Some attendees brought beautifully written letters.

As they presented their gifts, friends said a few words about each girl. "You have such a sweet and gentle spirit." "You are an amazing artist." "I feel so blessed to have you as my friend." These were some of the words offered to my daughter. Parents also spoke words of encouragement and praise to their child. All four of the young ladies were treated as princesses that evening. They glowed in the warmth of love showered upon them.

At the end, the four girls formed a circle in the middle of the room alongside a beloved teacher. She prayed God's blessing over each one of them. We all prayed along. It was the loveliest birthday party I have ever attended, and it brought tears of gratitude to my eyes.

The birthday party made me think. How often do I celebrate my children? Do they know how very much I love them? Do I tell them enough? How do I show them? Every child has special qualities and talents. Are they ever recognized? Do they know they are precious? Am I more their critic or their cheerleader? Do I celebrate their victories, however small?

From that day forward, I resolved to do better. I pledged to hug my children every day and tell them I love them. I planned to do more fun things with them. I vowed to stop criticizing my daughter for wearing colorful outfits and wacky hairdos. I would give my son the solitude he needed. I promised to stop constantly advising both of them. They did not have to be exactly like me. I wanted to be more generous with praise. I would allow them to make mistakes and say nothing. I cannot change anyone else, but I prayed God would help change me.

"Not all of us can do great things. But we can do small things with great love."

Mother Teresa

Chapter Fourteen
Lend a Helping Hand

About a dozen churches and synagogues in our area take turns hosting homeless families. For a week at a time, four times during the year, our church sets up bedrooms in vacant Sunday School classrooms. Several families (up to sixteen guests) reside with us for that week. Each family has a private room where they can all stay together. The congregation provides beds, tables, sheets, towels, toiletries, and home-cooked meals. Different Sunday School classes sign up to provide the dinners. There is a centrally located family center where they can wash clothes, watch television, use a computer, and take showers. Our local YMCA provides complimentary passes as well. The purpose of this nonprofit is to help the homeless find jobs, eliminate debt, and save money so they can eventually afford their own apartments. The program has been successful. Most participants save money and are living in their own homes within six months.

Our family helps serve meals occasionally. We enjoy visiting with the guests. As a volunteer, I never asked our guests personal questions, but one evening a lady shared her story with me. Until recently, this single mom had worked as an accountant. Then she was laid off. She found a lower- paying job, but could not keep up with a mortgage payment, medical and other bills, and a large student loan debt. She eventually lost her home. She and two children were living in their car until she heard about this community program.

I learned that many of the homeless are willing to work and provide for their families but need temporary assistance. Some are ill and have huge medical bills. Others are drowning in debt. Some are divorced and not receiving child support. Spending time with these neighbors gave me a whole new perspective. I finally realized anyone can find themselves without a place to live.

Is helping others important to your family? What do you enjoy doing when it comes to community service? If you are interested in volunteer work, there are many nonprofits to consider.

Fellow homeschoolers told our family about many opportunities to lend a hand. At first, I thought I was too busy and that anything I did wouldn't make much of a difference. I finally realized that, although our family couldn't solve all the world's problems, we could do something small. We could serve meals, clean up, help with a canned food drive, or recycle litter. Together with other volunteers, our group could accomplish what needed to be done in our community. Community service eventually became part of our educational program.

How many times have God and others blessed me? My husband had eye surgery and friends brought dinner for two weeks. They donated money when he couldn't work for a month. I had cancer surgery and they brought food and cleaned my house. Older students at the home studies learning center offered to tutor Katie. Members of our co-op and the country school took my children on a number of field trips. Such kindnesses are too numerous to name. We all need help from time to time. Sometimes, we are able to give back.

You may want to visit your local chamber of commerce website to see the nonprofits in your area. Homeschoolsuccess .com shows you how to integrate volunteer activities into your homeschool program. Or you may find plenty of volunteer opportunities at a local church, synagogue or community center.

"I believe that God put us in
this jolly world to be happy
and enjoy life."

Robert Baden-Powell

Chapter Fifteen
Relax and Enjoy the Journey

It was a beautiful morning in early January. I watched one of the most gorgeous sunrises I had ever seen. The azure sky was filled with pink and coral-colored clouds. They drifted above a deep blue, gold-flecked sea. I stood on my hotel balcony, eight floors above a Florida beach, looking out over the Atlantic Ocean and thinking there was no place I'd rather be. I inhaled the fresh salty air and listened to the seagulls squawking. In a few minutes, I would stroll along the water's edge, looking for shells and hoping to glimpse some dolphins. It was the first month of the new year and I was ready to make a fresh start.

My husband owns a small business and January is his slowest month. So, during the first month of every year, our family drives down to south Florida. I love coming home to the land where I was raised. The beach is my happy place. On such a lovely and quiet morning, I knew that God was in His heaven and all was right with the world.

Homeschooling allowed us the opportunity to travel whenever we liked. In most of the U.S., January is cold and snow covers the ground. Children are back in school, seated at their desks, keeping inside to stay warm. But we were at the beach, enjoying bright blue skies and balmy breezes. We were no longer restricted by school schedules.

I spent too much time worrying instead of relaxing. Why did I get so caught up in checking items off my to-do list? Why was I concerned my children wouldn't excel on their SATs? Did they really have to ace chemistry next year? Would they ever be the most popular kids at school? Roy's grandmother was a teacher and the mother of a child with special needs. She gave me great advice when Katie was first diagnosed with autism. "Relax," she said, "and enjoy spending time with your daughter."

Vacations are a great time to take it easy, but I finally figured out it's important to relax and have fun every day. So I taught classes outside. My children and I took walks through the woods and identified leaves and birds. We went swimming, entertained friends, or worked on a puzzle. Sometimes, we repurposed scraps of wood or created mosaics. We baked cookies and we painted. We were learning to enjoy life wherever we were.

There are a number of homeschool websites about relaxing and letting go of stress. Two sites, which I have not yet mentioned, are therelaxedhomeschool.com and lifeofahomeschoolmom.com. It is so easy to worry when you're a homeschool parent. I often told myself that no one is perfect and worrying has never accomplished anything.

"Life has loveliness to sell,
all beautiful and splendid things,
blue waves whitened on a cliff,
soaring fire that sways and sings,
and children's faces looking up,
holding wonder like a cup."

Sara Teasdale

Chapter Sixteen
Glimpsing God's Grandeur

There are times in life when I am simply awed. The days spent holding my newborn babies. When I sat on the rim of the Grand Canyon at sunset and the vibrantly colored rocks seemed to melt. Seeing the turquoise water and pink sand of Bermuda's beaches. My first glimpse of the Swiss Alps. Walking in the Colorado Rockies with three feet of pure white snow against a clear sapphire sky. These glimpses of God's grandeur bring tears to my eyes and ignite my soul. I feel as though I can't hold any more beauty than this, that my soaring spirit can climb no higher. I am truly grateful.

We traveled far to see some incredible sights, but there is beauty everywhere. There are wondrous things that I overlook every day. Like the sunset in my own backyard. My children's smiles. A mama bird feeding her babies. A hydrangea bush bursting with pink and blue blooms. A red tail hawk flying overhead.

Katie has a gift for noticing things that others miss, for finding beauty in the mundane. Perhaps it is her artist's eye that picks up on the lovely shape and design of a pine cone or the unique patterns in tree bark. She recognizes that even the dirt and the rocks in our yard sparkle in the sunlight. Her attention to detail is extraordinary. Her drawings reflect life through the lens of Asperger's and her faith in God. She's taught me to see our world differently and appreciate it more.

One day, I noticed Katie sitting on the bench swing in our back yard, deep in prayer. I asked her later what she had prayed about and she said, "I was telling God what a wonderful life I have."

Homeschooling gave Katie more time to be outdoors, to experience the solace and beauty of nature. In our back yard or at the park or beside the lake, she could quiet her soul and take time to observe our wonderful world. She spent many afternoons doing just that, with her sketch book beside her.

Bobby also enjoyed being outside. He loved the peace and quiet. He thought more clearly in solitude. He had a strong desire to keep our beautiful planet clean, so my son picked up litter and recycled plastic bottles. He had a yard-work business and he saw beauty in a well-maintained lawn. Those small things brought him joy.

What brings your child joy? What does she spend her free time doing? What does she tell you she wants to do? Noodle .com advises how to turn that interest into a curriculum your child will truly enjoy.

"Scouting rises within you
and inspires you to put
forth your best."

Juliette Gordon Low

Chapter Seventeen
Scouting and Other Extracurricular Activities

A crowd of nearly 40,000 gathered in Turner Field on September 29, 2012. The Braves were playing the New York Mets, and Chipper Jones was retiring at the end of the season. My husband and I stood just above the dugout to watch our daughter. Camera poised, I held my breath as Katie and eighteen other members of the 100th Anniversary Girl Scout Chorus marched proudly onto the field to sing the national anthem. Miss Georgia accompanied them to sign as the girls sang.

On March 10, 2013, I sat with hundreds in the Egyptian Ballroom of the Fox Theater. The audience stood as the song "Girl on Fire" blared through the auditorium. Katie and 112 other Girl Scout Gold Award recipients from all over Georgia paraded down the aisle to the front of the stage. The Gold Award is the highest award that can be earned in Girl Scouting and requires 100 hours of service. During the ceremony, each honoree's name appeared overhead followed by her personal statement. Katie wrote, "I feel like I accomplished a lot and I am excited. I loved seeing the students' creativity blossom! I really enjoyed teaching the kids in my art classes."

We watched with interest as each young women was recognized for her community service. One girl started a nonprofit and shipped 3000 books to an orphanage in Kenya. Another assembled more than 1000 care packages for children's hospitals. A third organized and held a pageant for special needs teenagers. One Scout started a fitness program for the intellectually disabled and another young woman dug wells in India. One amazing project followed another. We enthusiastically applauded these high school girls. They were changing the world.

Katie offered free art classes for elementary school children in our community. She spent weeks advertising, planning lessons, and collecting art supplies. My daughter also invited local artists to help teach the classes. At the end of the fall semester, she organized an art show to display the students' work.

This project greatly helped Katie to stretch herself and get out of her comfort zone. Her social and communication skills were strengthened. Students and their parents were grateful for her efforts. Several of the children made thank-you cards for Katie. One mom told us her daughter never showed the slightest interest in art until Katie's class. Now, drawing is a part of her everyday routine. Jose said he liked it better than his art class at school. Laura wrote, "I'm such a good artist because of you." Edward's mom told us, "Edward loved the art classes. I could tell because he never complained about going."

On August 4, 2013, we again sat in a large theater to honor teenagers in our community. We were there to recognize Bobby and about 150 other Eagle Scouts. I nudged my husband as a picture of Bobby and his troop building a teaching platform for our church preschool appeared on the screen. We watched as dozens of pictures showed Eagle projects ranging from constructing a gazebo or garden to digging wells or starting schools overseas. One writer described the rank of Eagle Scout as the PhD of boyhood. Indeed, an amazing group of young men walked across the stage that afternoon. I was incredibly impressed with their accomplishments and wondered what each might achieve in adulthood.

Bobby summed up his Eagle experience in a college essay. Here is part of what he wrote, "I started Boy Scouts when I was nearly sixteen and finished with the rank of Eagle just before my eighteenth birthday. At times it was very stressful and hectic due to the fact that I only had two years to complete twenty-one merit badges, sixteen months of leadership, an Eagle project, and all the required community service hours. During eleventh grade, I was bombarded with homework and dual enrollment classes. There were times where I questioned my hopes and ability of ever accomplishing the Eagle in twenty-six months. There were people who even doubted it was possible. Fortunately, by God's grace and with very helpful troop leaders, I was able to pull through.

"The hardest part about my Eagle project was deciding what to do. I had several decent project ideas, but those fell through. I became discouraged and started to lose hope until God gave my pastor an idea which he shared with me. I built an outdoor teaching facility and the church was able to fund this, leaving me a relief from stress because I didn't have to raise a lot of money. Over twenty boys from my troop helped me build it while I supervised the construction with the help of my dad.

"To sum it all up, without God, I would not have stood a chance to accomplish a number of goals including Eagle Scout. God has blessed me with countless abstract and concrete things that we take for granted every second of the day. As strange as it may seem, God works through others in laying the building blocks of my life."

These three events are forever engraved on my heart. They are favorite scenes from the movie of our lives. Scouting played a huge part in my children's lives and was a very important part of their educational journey. Scouting taught them to work as part of a team and to never give up. Katie and Bobby learned how to select a goal, focus on it, and achieve it through hard work and determination. They discovered that, as part of a group, they could accomplish something they couldn't do alone. We were blessed with incredible leaders who encouraged, helped, and served as excellent role models. God's hand was evident throughout our time in Scouts. What would you like your child to achieve? What does your child enjoy? Where might he or she excel?

There are many benefits to extracurricular activities. I am thankful there are a large number of groups open to homeschooled children. If your child is musical, there are homeschool bands, choirs, and city orchestra programs. For those who love sports, there are county and church baseball and basketball teams. Blog.collegevine.com provides a great guide to extracurriculars for homeschooled students. These activities include athletics, chess club, community service, debate team, drama, religious groups, public speaking, student government, writing, and performing arts. There are activities to suit any child. The many benefits include making friends, developing professional and life skills, gaining confidence, exploring interests, making a contribution, as well as learning time management and teamwork.

Another huge benefit is that students can include these activities on their college applications. Colleges want students who are well-rounded. With homeschooling, there are many opportunities to be just that.

"Children will not remember
you for the material things you
provided but for the feeling that
you cherished them."

Richard L. Evans

Chapter Eighteen
Family Frugality

Does it seem like there's never enough money to go around? Who can afford to homeschool?

It was the day before the homeschool used-book sale. I pulled into the church parking lot with five boxes filled with items I hoped to sell. Two teenaged boys carried my books into the church gym. Dozens of volunteers sorted them by subject and grade level and placed them on tables. During the next two days, hundreds attended this event and purchased thousands of textbooks, educational DVDs and games, and other homeschool necessities. The sellers got to keep 80% of their total sales. It was a great way to make money on items your children no longer needed and to save on next year's school supplies.

The book sale was one of many ways we saved money while homeschooling. We also saved by swapping books and sports equipment and by pooling resources. We bartered for services such as cleaning or babysitting in exchange for piano or art lessons. I taught classes in lieu of school tuition. We held garage sales. As a one-income family, we learned to save money any way we could.

Our budget was certainly stretched. Books are expensive and so are private art lessons. Then there are costs for supplies, standardized testing, transcript accreditation, field trips, sports, tutoring, and certain classes. At first, I felt overwhelmed by so many educational options and ended up spending way more than I intended. Unfortunately, homeschool expenses are not tax deductible. There is no voucher for home-educated students.

Thankfully, there are some inexpensive ways to teach and entertain children. Having a budget doesn't mean settling for a substandard education. We became creative and looked for affordable ways to provide educational experiences. I found a library book on homeschooling your child for free. There were complimentary days at museums, history and science centers, public gardens, and skating rinks. Libraries provided free programs and communities offered outdoor concerts, street fairs, and craft shows. We also attended free performances, lectures, and art galleries at local colleges. We had picnics, took hikes, or rode our bicycles at state parks. We went to the Georgia state capitol building and visited animal shelters. We learned how to be frugal, have fun, and still get a great education.

There are several websites offering free activities for homeschoolers including homeschool.com and homeschoolsuccess.com. Local newspapers and community magazines also list free events.

Debt is not anyone's friend. I wish I had learned this lesson prior to college, before I maxed out my credit cards and accumulated a mountain of student loan debt. Thankfully, our homeschool co-op offered personal finance classes for high school students. Teenagers learned how to balance a checkbook, file a tax return, shop at thrift stores, and use coupons in the grocery store. These students learned how to save thousands of dollars by taking free college courses while in high school, under our state scholarship program. They learned how to save money and say no to loans.

Daveramsey.com offers great advice on managing money, including a helpful article titled "Five Things Your Teenager Needs to Know Before College."

One day I tagged along as the personal finance teacher took her students to a thrift store. Each one of them had a budget of thirty dollars. Clothes were 75% off on Wednesdays, so they were able to fill their shopping carts with designer jeans and shirts. Many garments were in great condition. Some of the T-shirts and shorts were only a quarter. Bobby needed more of these for his part-time job. Who wants to spend a lot of money on clothes to do yard work? Katie selected clothes she could wear while painting. She even found some cute shoes for a dollar.

Two students were headed to college in the fall and wanted to furnish their dorm rooms. They found chairs and small bookshelves for a few dollars each. After a coat of paint, they would look great. This group of students was saving their money for college or a car. Matthew wanted to make a down payment on a house. Most of them worked part-time and knew firsthand the value of a dollar. We were all amazed at what you can buy in a thrift store, even on a very limited budget.

Websites about saving money when homeschooling include joyinthehome.com, moneycrashers.com/homeschool-child-budget/ (How to Homeschool Your Child on a Budget & Save Money), and workingathomeschool.com. There are plenty of ways to stretch your budget. Be creative.

"Nothing in this world can take the place of persistence. Talent will not; nothing is more common than unsuccessful men with talent. Genius will not; unrewarded genius is almost a proverb. Education will not; the world is full of educated derelicts. Persistence and determination alone are omnipotent."

Calvin Coolidge

Chapter Nineteen
Dual Enrollment and College Preparation

We sat in a large conference room with over 100 high school seniors, all of whom had participated in Georgia's "Move on When Ready" or dual enrollment program. Most had attended public or private schools, but about a dozen were homeschooled. These seniors would soon graduate with earned college credits. Our state offers free college tuition to high school students with a 3.0 GPA and qualifying SAT or ACT scores. Since the local college Bobby attended was accredited by the Southern Association of Colleges and Schools (SACS), these credits would transfer to any university in the country. We felt incredibly blessed.

Roy and I watched as Bobby was called forward to receive a medal and a certificate. He completed ten core classes, including college algebra and world history, to earn thirty college credit hours. This program would save our family thousands of dollars! Bobby started dual enrollment in his junior year, but we knew students who qualified in the ninth grade. Tom would graduate from high school with forty-five college credit hours and enter the honors program at the University of Georgia as a sophomore. We all applauded as Hannah, a homeschooled friend, was recognized for maintaining a 4.0 college GPA during two years of dual enrollment. She had been accepted to several top universities. Whoever said home study doesn't prepare young people for college?

Georgia offers tuition-free dual enrollment programs for high school students as well as a HOPE (Helping Outstanding Pupils Educationally) scholarship for qualifying college students. Other states may not. If you are interested, there is a wealth of information available on the internet. There you will find answers to such questions as requirements for dual enrollment, whether these classes affect college GPA and whether AP classes are better than dual enrollment. You can also find out which colleges in your state participate in this program, if there are scholarships available, and how to apply. The admission requirements differ for each academic institution. Georgia students may look at gafutures.org, or gadoe.org for program information and an application. A homeschool learning center may have an administrator who will help you or you may visit your local college for assistance. You might also ask a homeschool parent who has a child in the dual enrollment program for advice.

I shared this information with a homeschool mom and she told me her thirteen-year-old son would never qualify. He had a learning disability. He had taken a practice SAT test and done very poorly. I assured her that he could do it. He was smart and he still had several years to prepare. He could practice answering SAT questions online or in a study book. He could read SAT vocabulary cartoons and take SAT and ACT prep classes. He could watch Khan Academy math tutorials and read books that contained hundreds of SAT vocabulary words. There were many ways to prepare and no reason to give up hope so quickly.

I told this mom about my children's struggles with both the SAT and the ACT. They took the SAT first and did not do well. They took the ACT and did somewhat better. Since the ACT was their preferred test, they took it several times, hoping for better scores. Bobby then qualified to enter dual enrollment at several local schools. Katie did not qualify at first. Her math score was quite good, but she could not score any higher than 18 in English and she needed at least a 19. She could barely finish two-thirds of the test before her time was up. Like some on the autism spectrum, she was above average in certain areas, but struggled in language arts. She also needed additional time to process information.

I asked a friend for help. She told me that the local two-year college offered a test called the Accuplacer. The great advantage was that students had considerably more time to take it. Katie took this test, did very well, and gained admittance to the school's dual enrollment program. She went on to earn all As and Bs at this school and these credits transferred to a selective four-year college after high school graduation.

When it comes to standardized testing to qualify for dual enrollment, don't give up easily. Give your child a fair chance to succeed. We told Katie that there's no disgrace in failing, as long as you do your best, but it's a shame if you don't even try. Khanacademy.org offers free SAT practice tests and so does collegereadiness.collegeboard.org. Persistence is an important quality for successful students and an essential one for the homeschooling parent. The most significant thing I learned during my homeschooling experience was the importance of persistence.

If you have a high school student who is preparing for college, you will find helpful tips at usnews.com/education/

best-colleges/slideshows/10-ways-to-prepare-for-your-freshman-year-of-college. Their advice includes read as much as possible, grow your technical skill set, polish your people skills, embrace time-management tools, and know where to go for academic help. Professionals.collegeboard.org is another good website. They recommend taking more challenging high school courses, doing well on standardized tests, and being involved in extracurricular activities. This advice applies to homeschoolers as well as private school or public school students.

College is not for everyone. But don't rule it out just because your child is on the autism spectrum. Most colleges offer support services for students with disabilities. A two-year college might be a good place for your child to start.

"Congratulations!
Today is your day.
You're off to great places!
You're off and away!"

Dr. Seuss

Chapter Twenty
Bobby's High School Graduation

Their lives literally flashed before our eyes. The lives of fifteen graduating seniors appeared on the large screen above the stage. We watched a slide show for every graduate, beginning with baby pictures and ending with a formal graduation portrait. We saw significant moments from the eighteen years they had spent on this earth. A picture of puppies made us laugh and the one of a mission trip to Africa touched us deeply.

Following the slide show, all of the graduates from our co-op performed a skit. Then some sang, danced, or played a musical instrument. Two of them shared their favorite homeschooling stories with the audience. Finally, when each senior's name was called, their parents joined them on stage. I handed Bobby his diploma and he gave me a bouquet of flowers. This was a treasured moment to be captured on film and remembered forever.

In the church reception hall, each graduate had their own table filled with items of great sentimental value. There were trophies, art work, baseball gloves, Eagle Scout memorabilia, scrapbooks, and hundreds of photos on display. There were pictures of family and friends, of overseas mission trips and vacations taken around the world. This high school graduation ceremony was the loveliest one I have ever attended.

By God's grace, I had actually homeschooled Katie and Bobby through high school. They had greatly enjoyed the opportunity to meet and study with almost two hundred homeschooled students during their middle school and high school years. They made close friends and became an active part of their community. They were grateful for their educational journey. We had wonderful memories of these formative years. They had both been accepted to half a dozen selective colleges.

I must admit, I had mixed feelings when my children graduated from high school. I asked God if I might hold on to this moment when we're all healthy, happy, safe, and together. I thanked God for giving them wings to soar, but I hoped they'd stay perched for just a little while longer.

Most of their fellow homeschoolers from the co-op, the learning center, and the country school started college the fall after graduation. Bobby had an academic scholarship, and Tony was going to college on a golf scholarship. Several graduates could afford to attend a private school. Others would spend two years at a technical college. Bobby and Hannah had earned enough college credits to start as sophomores.

Some high school seniors know exactly what they want to do, but many do not. John's parents encouraged him to be a doctor because he excelled in science and math. He got into a very selective college. But he ran into problems when he failed organic chemistry. At that point, he realized he never really wanted to go into medicine. John's passion was flying and he actually wanted to become a Navy pilot. He began to wholeheartedly pursue his dream career.

Some graduates chose not to go right into college. Two of

the boys took a gap year. George worked at a restaurant and Daniel traveled for a few months. Jason and Steve started working in their family construction business. Cathy finished ballet school in New York City and joined a ballet company in California. Mandy spent a year as a missionary in the Philippines. Kyle and David went into the military and served overseas. Diane traveled the world performing before being admitted to a prestigious music school. Yolonda opened her own photography studio. Jack was a fifth-degree black belt and decided to manage a karate studio. They are all God's masterpieces and He has a great plan for their lives.

Bobby's graduation ceremony demonstrated the essence of homeschooling. For what is the purpose of education if not to help each individual reach their full potential? Isn't it to celebrate the unique gifts and attributes of each student? To help them find their God-given purpose and prepare them for adulthood? Homeschooling allowed our family and many others the precious opportunity to do just that. It allowed them to spend much of their time pursuing their passions and developing their talents. It opened students' minds to the fact that all things are possible with faith.

"Twenty years from now, you will be more disappointed by the things you didn't do than by the ones you did do. So, throw off the bowlines. Sail away from the safe harbor. Catch the trade winds in your sails. Explore, Dream, Discover."

Mark Twain

Chapter Twenty-One
Katie Goes to College

On a warm, sunny morning, Roy and I drove Katie up to college. Our car was filled with suitcases.

Bobby shook his head. "All she needs is her old bedspread, a couple outfits, and a pair of sneakers." The trip took two hours but it felt like a journey to a far distant land. This private Christian college has one of the most beautiful campuses we have ever seen. From the top of the mountain, there was a spectacular panoramic view of at least five states. There was also a gorgeous view from the dining hall and from Katie's dorm room.

That afternoon, Roy and I sat with other parents in front of a beautiful stained glass window in the college chapel. We joined the college president and the dean in praying for the freshman class. I felt at peace. This was where Katie belonged. Later, we met her delightful roommate and some other new friends. But driving home that evening, I felt as though my life was stuck on fast forward. I wished I could hit the replay button. I missed Katie already.

Three months earlier, Katie graduated from the country school as the valedictorian in a class of eleven. In high school, she earned two national awards: the Girl Scout Gold Award and the President's Volunteer Service Award. She also received the Georgia Hope scholarship, which provides free tuition to students with qualifying grades and test scores. She went from a special education student with a full-time paraprofessional to the recipient of two scholarships at a selective college. God is good and homeschooling works!

What is your vision for your child? What hopes do you have for his or her future? Do they want to attend college? How can you best prepare them? Parentingaspergerscommunity.com and childmind.org offer advice on how to help a child with Asperger's prepare for college.

"Never spend your money
before you have it."

Thomas Jefferson

Chapter Twenty-Two
College Costs

One of my most embarrassing moments occurred when I was a graduate student. Ten of us decided to canoe across the ocean from the North Carolina coast to the Outer Banks. It was a gorgeous spring evening when we paddled out on a calm sea to a small deserted island. We pulled our canoes up on the beach, set up tents, built a campfire, and made dinner. We went to sleep just as it started to rain.

Early the next morning, we discovered that all but one of our canoes had been swept away by the nighttime thunderstorm. Thankfully, the one remaining canoe held some food and water. We set out in search of the other boats. We waded across to a neighboring island and found one canoe caught in the rocks. The others had probably been carried out to sea.

By late afternoon, there was no food and we were about out of water. We had not seen anyone else and began to panic. Together, we continued to walk and wade through the shallow part of the sea. The sun beat down. We breathed heavily, inhaling the salty air. Finally, we reached a cove and spotted a small fishing boat in the distance. We yelled, but they were too far away to hear us.

Jim and Heidi grabbed a large white blanket from the first

canoe and waved it until they caught the fishermen's attention. The men headed our way, but shallow, rocky waters prevented their boat from reaching us. About an hour later, we were finally rescued by the Coast Guard. I wonder if the locals are still chuckling about the college kids who were dumb enough to canoe across the ocean and then didn't even have the sense to tie up their boats.

So I know how it feels to be up the creek (or out in the ocean) without a paddle (or my boat). This was the same feeling I had when my children were accepted to several colleges and I looked at the costs of attending. I had focused only on preparing them for college. I also should have thought about how we were going to pay for it. We had some money set aside, but not nearly enough. Katie and Bobby were offered academic scholarships, but we still couldn't afford for both to be at private schools costing $40,000 to over $50,000 a year. I should have started saving for college when they were babies.

How can anyone afford college? Should we take out student loans? That's what I had done. But Bobby and Katie had completed Dave Ramsey's *Foundations in Personal Finance: Home School Student Text*. Ramsey asks if it is worth borrowing $75,000 to go to an expensive private school when you can attend a local college and pay for it with cash. Bobby was accepted to several great schools in California, but did not want to graduate owing $80,000. He figured that would be a monthly student loan payment of $800 for ten years. A future finance major, Bobby opted to attend the local state university. With scholarships, he could earn a four-year degree for a grand total of $12,000. I should have been so smart.

Katie loved the private college, but decided to transfer to the local university her sophomore year. It was much more affordable. They also offered a degree in architecture and she had been accepted into that program.

There are a number of websites on obtaining college scholarships. Great scholarship search engines include scholarships.com, collegeboard.org, and Fastweb.com. CBSNews.com offers "10 Great Ways to Win a College Scholarship." They state that students who volunteer have a huge advantage. Another great piece of advice is to think local. These scholarships will be easier to win.

Start saving for college as early as possible. I wish I had.

"Bless the LORD, O my soul, and forget not all His benefits."

Psalm 103:2 KJV

Chapter Twenty-Three
Remembering

Roy, Katie, and I were turning onto the highway when we heard a loud explosion. About thirty yards ahead of us, one car had hit another with such force that the second vehicle was knocked off the highway and halfway up the embankment. A former EMT, Roy rushed over to help. Already he was fearing the worst. He had arrived at similar crashes where no one survived. Another witness immediately called for an ambulance.

As first responders, he and another man pulled a lady and four small children out of the car. Smoke billowed out from the vehicle, so they needed to do this. Roy carried a baby girl out and placed her in her mother's arm. This girl did not have a scratch on her! The driver's door would not open, but the man assured Roy he was okay. So was the man driving the other car. Miraculously, all seven of the people involved in the accident survived with no serious injuries!

Paramedics arrived a few minutes later. A little boy had a gash across his forehead, but they said he should be fine. The other children were completely unharmed. The accident reminded me that life is fragile and a precious gift from God. Tragedies can happen in an instant and we constantly need His protection.

Have you ever witnessed a miracle? Have you known without a doubt that God protected you or a loved one from disaster?

I write to record and remember what God has done. Among my most treasured possessions are photo albums and journals going back to my teenage years. Every year, around Christmas, I look back through my diary and remember of all of God's blessings during the past twelve months. I write down these gifts from Him and His answers to prayer, so I won't forget. They may be life-or-death events or merely small winks from God. Sometimes you don't see the significance of a moment until long after it has passed.

God's goodness was evident throughout our homeschooling years and beyond. He provided fantastic teachers and mentors who inspired a passion for learning. He gave us opportunities to learn and grow alongside wonderful families. He led my children to outstanding Scout troops that instilled confidence and a desire to serve. He brought us friends who loved and accepted Katie and Bobby. We had plenty of opportunities to travel. God helped us and was with us, even during the most challenging times.

Is homeschooling right for your child? What is best depends on the individual. I know young people who excelled in public school, those who thrived in private school, and others who blossomed with homeschooling. Every child is different, and you know your child better than anyone. How can your unique child reach his or her full potential? What do you hope your child will learn and remember? Are you willing to be the primary teacher? Homeschooling was a great fit for our family. Will it be for yours?

I think back to the question the school counselor asked me over a decade ago, "Don't you want her to be like everyone else?"

Katie is not perfect and neither am I. Everyone has strengths and weaknesses. But God's power and goodness are evident in spite of our shortcomings. I look again at my resilient, courageous, and persistent daughter who has overcome Asperger's and so much more. She is hopeful, smart, beautiful, and one of a kind.

My answer is now a resounding no!

About the Author

Elizabeth Bauman is a retired teacher who holds a M.Ed. from UNC-Chapel Hill. She homeschooled both of her children through middle and high school. Elizabeth and her daughter co-authored two children's picture books, *Hope's Colors* and *Homeschooling Hope.* They donate a portion of the proceeds to Autism Speaks. Her vision is to help homeschooled children, including those on the autism spectrum, reach their full potential. Her two children participated in Georgia's Move On When Ready/dual enrollment program and both received HOPE scholarships. Her son is an Eagle Scout who earned a BBA in finance. Her daughter is a college senior and the recipient of the Girl Scout Gold Award and the President's Volunteer Service Award.

Connect with Elizabeth Bauman at TreasuredAndTeachable.wordpress.com

If You Enjoyed This Book Consider Sharing It

- Please mention the book on Facebook, Twitter, Pinterest, or your blog
- Recommend this book to your small group, book club, or workplace
- Pick up a copy for someone you know who would be helped or encouraged by this message
- Write a review on Amazon.com

98380536R00078

Made in the USA
Columbia, SC
26 June 2018